MELBA AND ME

Queens of the Mountain

WRITTEN BY SUSAN B. KLUSMAN

ILLUSTRATED BY JOHN COLES

ISBN: Softcover   978-1-9845-2583-3
        Hardcover   978-1-9845-2582-6
        EBook   978-1-9845-2584-0

Print information available on the last page

Rev. date: 06/05/2018

To order additional copies of this book, contact:
Xlibris
1-888-795-4274
www.Xlibris.com
Orders@Xlibris.com

Melba and *Me* is dedicated to my family and Melba's family.

FOREWORD

When I was about eight years old, my family built a cabin in the foothills of the Sierra Nevada in Carson Valley. We were several miles from Genoa, the oldest town in Nevada, with a population of seventy-five. South Lake Tahoe was on the other side of the mountains. We actually lived in San Rafael, California, and drove about four hours to enjoy our holidays and most of the summers at our cabin.

My friend Melba's last name was Filmore. Her family sold an acre of their land to my family to build our cabin. The following vignettes are my memories with Melba. She and her mother lived in a small house about a mile below ours. These stories stand out from a backdrop of azure skies, hot dry weather (that was cooler in the shade), snakes, especially rattlesnakes, and cold winters when we were at times snowed in. Melba and I occasionally went down in the valley to play with some children who lived on the farms. However, the following adventures are the ones I treasure.

ABOUT MELBA

Melba and I were neighbors, although we lived about a mile apart from each other. Our houses were the only two on the mountainside. There really were three houses altogether, but the Bruggemann family rarely used their house. They lived in the city.

The tallest mountain, Job's Peak, towered far above our houses. Right below its pointed peak stood a ridge which resembled a question mark. During the spring you could see the mark clearly when the snow stayed on the side of the mountain face and the snow on the question mark melted away. When we were in the valley below, we looked for Job's Peak to locate our houses on the mountainside.

Our homes were hard to spot from the valley. They were small, and their colors blended into the colors of the landscape. My house was grey matching the sagebrush bushes. Melba's house was pale-green blending in with the green tea bushes and pine trees. Her house was below mine. So, I would run down the hill to see her.

Melba and her mother lived in their one-room house. They were members of the Washoe Indian tribe. Melba had two dogs that explored the mountainside with us: two independent and curious girls.

THE CREEK

The water in the creek that ran straight down the mountain near our houses was very cold. We believed that the water came from the snow that melted during the spring time. Melba and I created a path from my house to her house along the creek. The path wound its way through the trees and crossed the creek several times. We jumped across the creek in some spots, or we walked on slippery stones in other areas. I don't think we ever fell. The white trees that grew near the creek were not very tall, and the rocks were not big either. We felt like everything was our size, and we could run quickly up or down our path undetected.

Rainbow trout swam down the creek. Sometimes Melba and I would make fishing poles out of the branches of the trees. We would attach a string to one end of the branch and tie some bread on the end of the dangling string and sit with our string in the water waiting to catch a fish. We watched them swim past our baited string but never caught one.

We did figure out a way to catch them. We found a narrow part of the creek which we each straddled and waited until a fish came through the narrow passageway. Then we would scoop the fish up with our bare hands and fling it onto the bank where it would flop around. It was tricky to catch the slippery fish. Then, whoever had the longest shirt tail would wrap the ends around the fish. We would slowly walk home with the wriggling fish. We didn't catch fish this way often; it seemed to take all day.

Swimming in the creek was chilly. We only got the idea when we were really hot. Just sitting near the water would cool us off. If we took our shoes and socks off and put our toes in, it cooled us enough. There were days, however, when we just felt like getting wet all over. The water was not deep and only came up to our knees. It was so clear we could easily see our toenails on the clean white sand, but so cold we had to dare each other to go in farther. We could only get completely wet in a small pool we found. The pool was so narrow we could only stretch out one way, the way the water was running down. If we finally did lay down with our head sticking up, our chests would hurt because of the cold, and we would quickly jump out.

Finding out where the creek began was a goal we had often when choosing which route to take up the mountain. We would start out early in the morning, walk up over large granite boulders, through groups of trees following the creek. By the afternoon, another spot away from the creek would often capture our attention, and we would abandon our idea of finding the creek's source. Though we never found the source, we never tired trying to do so.

THE MINE

On other days we would climb to the abandoned mine which was up the mountain, far from the creek. It usually took all day. We always packed a lunch when we went exploring. The mine was not very big. The entrance was blocked by fallen logs. It looked like only one person had mined there. From the entrance there was a small mound of small pink, white, and grey rocks which had been discarded and had flowed several feet down the mountain. We could sit side by side pushing our bottoms slowly sliding down the mountain through the little pink rocks looking for quartz crystals. The crystals we found were small. Some were smoky colored and others were clear. Once I found a fat, clear one the size of my thumb.

Sometimes as we were sliding down from the mine, we would stop about midway and examine the valley below. We could see large and small parcels of land divided up by the color of the crops. Here and there in the corner of a field were clusters of trees where the farmhouses stood. The valley was so vast we could barely see the mountains on the other side where the pine nut trees grew. Billows of dust meant the farmers were using their tractors.

High up where we were perched, it was very quiet. The air was still. We felt part of the sky. When puffs of orange from the setting sun colored the blue sky or when we heard the ringing of the cow bell (a signal from my house to come home), we knew it was time to leave the mine.

THE PORCUPINE

Melba's two dogs had their own distinct personalities. Sport was black and white with long silky hair and he was friendly. Pig did not like being petted. His white hair was so short his pink skin showed through, and his tiny tail curlicued--he really looked like a pig! Sport and Pig would, when they felt like it, come exploring with us.

They were fairly good at killing scorpions. With their lips rolled back, they snatched up a scorpion with their teeth, shook their heads, threw the scorpions to the ground, watched to see if they squirmed, and if they moved, they picked them up again until finally the scorpions lay still.

One day when Sport and Pig came along, Melba and I found a cluster of small trees, about our size. The other trees on the mountainside were very tall pine trees. This little patch had smaller trees with delicate branches with soft oval leaves. We felt cozy sitting on a small boulder surrounded by the trees and dappled sunlight. Suddenly, Sport and Pig started barking excitedly. They were barking at a porcupine. We tried to pull them away from the porcupine, but they would not leave the animal alone. Sure enough, soon Sport and Pig were squealing. They had a bunch of porcupine quills sticking out around their snouts. Melba and I started to cry. All four of us ran down the mountain. Melba took Sport and Pig to her house.

A few hours later while I was sitting on my porch, I saw Pig walking towards my house. He had never come visiting before. With porcupine quills sprouting out of his muzzle, I knew he wanted me to help him. I got pliers and began pulling out the quills. He whined and winced while I was pulling but allowed me to get out most of the quills. After that experience, I liked Pig. He trusted me.

When they felt better, Sport and Pig came exploring with us again.

SLEEPING IN TREES

Now and then on a clear night, Melba and I would take sleeping bags, find a clearing, a patch of white sandy ground surrounded by sagebrush, and sleep outside. We brought yellow plastic cereal bowls, milk in a jar, which we put in the creek to keep cold, spoons, and small boxes of cereal for breakfast. When we were snug in our bags, we looked up at the clear, midnight-blue sky and talked about the many twinkling stars. In the distance coyotes would howl us to sleep.

One night we decided to sleep in a tall pine tree. This idea didn't turn out as we planned. We chose a tree that was easy to climb and had thick branches. We climbed the tree hauling up our sleeping bags. We each chose a branch and tried to get comfortable. We tried every which way to sleep but couldn't because we were afraid we would fall out of the tree as soon as we fell asleep. It was dark and we were tired. So, we climbed down and placed our bags near the trunk on top of pine needles and waited for sleep to come. Instead of sleeping, we jumped out of our bags frantically scratching off big black ants. We had forgotten about those ants that hid in the pine needles near the base of the trees. We ran up the hill with our bags to my porch where we finally slept. We never again tried sleeping in or even near a pine tree.

MAKING BASKETS

Melba's mother made baskets. She used the branches and roots of the youngest trees that grew by the creek. Sometimes Melba and I would quietly sit with her and watch. Her black hair was pulled back in one long braid that fell to her waist. She sat on the ground hunched over her work with the small bundles of branches and roots nearby.

She deftly cut the roots and branches with a pocket knife and pulled them through holes she made in the top part of a tin can. This way they would all be the same width. The branches were a tan color and the roots were dark brown. She used the roots for the designs which she wove into the basket and the branches were for the actual basket.

Melba's mother showed us how to weave spoons from the green tea bushes. The weaving took a lot of time and effort. We never finished a spoon, but they were fun to start. Melba's mother would also make tea for us from the bushes during the early summer. The stems had small cones on them at other times of the year. She would pick the new stems, put them in her apron, and then place them in a pot of boiling water. When the water became a brownish green, she poured it through a sieve to exclude the needles, and then we would drink it. It tasted a little bitter.

THE TEEPEE PEOPLE

One year the *teepee people* moved in across the creek, a short distance up the mountain from my house. They were not Indians. We called them the *teepee people* only because they lived in a teepee. We always were careful to walk far around their teepee when we went exploring.

One day, however, we were curious and decided to study them and their surroundings. We hid behind a sagebrush bush then crept to another bush, slowly making our way closer and closer to the teepee. We got so close that two small children spotted us. Their mother and father asked us to come inside and visit with them. There was a small fire in the middle of the teepee and blankets for us to sit on. They were cooking something over the fire and offered us some. It tasted like beef jerky. They said they had moved from the city. Outside they showed us how they cooked on stones. They ground corn and wheat on a rock that looked like a big bowl. They made a table out of logs and had a rock oven. After the short tour, we said thank-you and good-bye. We ran all the way home embarrassed we had been caught spying. We didn't visit them again.

When the first snow flakes began to fall, the *teepee people* returned to the city. The teepee stood tall throughout the winter; but one spring day, it was gone and so were they. Melba and I looked around the abandoned area and saw the stone cooking area, the only trace that they were ever there. We were glad they had left.

Once again, the mountain belonged to us.

MELBA

Melba was a bit older than I was. One day Melba took me to a small clearing in the woods that her family had chosen as her special place. The small piece of land was a lasting marker for Melba having grown up. She said she was a young woman now. Our mountain was a fitting witness to her occasion. Soon she and her mother moved away.

Afterword

I don't know where Melba and her mother moved to. After Melba left I was in my teenage years and less interested in exploring the mountainside. We both had new lives. The times we spent together were special; but, in retrospect they seem so brief, maybe several months each year for about three or four years.

Melba's mother made my brother a deerskin vest. She tanned a deer hide. She sewed on colorful beads for the designs. She gave it to him when he became a young man. She also made him a four-inch belt of colorful beads. She gave my parents a bowl and plate she made from the willows.

In sixth grade I did a project on the Washoe Indians and learned about Dat So La Lee, a famous basket weaver in Washoe Valley who was one of the first to use pitch to waterproof her baskets. I subsequently learned that the Washoe did use the green bushes, *Ephedra californica*, for making tea and for other medicinal purposes. They also used the stems to make utensils.

My family sold our cabin in the late 1960's. When I made a return visit many years later, I saw that the mountainside was littered with cabins each on their own half acre. A four-lane highway, Kingsbury Grade, scars the mountainside from South Lake Tahoe to Foothill Road near the houses. I learned that much of the mountainside once belonged to the Filmore's. As members of the Washoe Indian tribe, Melba's family was given a parcel of land on these foothills. Through the years the family sold the land.

Printed in the United States
By Bookmasters